Sure Foundations

Sure Foundations

Reflections on the Beginnings of Christianity

BRETT KNOWLES

RESOURCE *Publications* · Eugene, Oregon

SURE FOUNDATIONS
Reflections on the Beginnings of Christianity

Copyright © 2025 Brett Knowles. All rights reserved. Except for brief quotations in critical publications or reviews, no part of this book may be reproduced in any manner without prior written permission from the publisher. Write: Permissions, Wipf and Stock Publishers, 199 W. 8th Ave., Suite 3, Eugene, OR 97401.

Resource Publications
An Imprint of Wipf and Stock Publishers
199 W. 8th Ave., Suite 3
Eugene, OR 97401

www.wipfandstock.com

PAPERBACK ISBN: 979-8-3852-7084-2
HARDCOVER ISBN: 979-8-3852-7085-9
EBOOK ISBN: 979-8-3852-7086-6

VERSION NUMBER 121025

Cover photograph
Foto Ad Meskens. Edinburgh Castle as seen from Princes Street Gardens, Edinburgh, 4 September 2010. Wikipedia Commons, https://commons.wikimedia.org/wiki/File:Edinburgh_Castle_17.jpg. File cropped at bottom of picture. Creative Commons: https://creativecommons.org/licenses/by-sa/3.0/deed.en.

Scripture taken from the HOLY BIBLE, NEW INTERNATIONAL VERSION®. Copyright © 1973, 1978, 1984 by International Bible Society. Used by permission of Zondervan Publishing House. All rights reserved.

Contents

Preface | vii
Acknowledgments | ix

Chapter 1
What is the evidence for Jesus? | 1

Chapter 2
The Resurrection and the Empty Tomb | 10

Chapter 3
Encounters with the Risen Jesus | 20

Chapter 4
The Role of the Holy Spirit | 27

Chapter 5
That was then, this is now . . . | 40

Bibliography | 47

Preface

- When the foundations are being destroyed, what can the righteous do? (Ps.11:3)
- I lay a stone in Zion, a tested stone, a precious cornerstone for a firm foundation . . . (Isa.28:16)
- For no one can lay any foundation other than the one already laid, which is Jesus Christ. (1 Cor.3:11)

ONE OF THE FEATURES of our present era has been a massive shift in, and rearrangement of, frameworks that had previously seemed fixed and immovable. The decline of the Western "Liberal World Order"; the decay of democracy and the plunge towards authoritarianism in the United States and elsewhere; and the changing networks of relationship between nations, all indicate that our current world is being swept off the foundations upon which it previously had stood.

Similarly, belief systems have been shaken, and Christianity has often been treated with scorn, being regarded as antiquated, anti-intellectual, and irrelevant. The rejection of religious conviction as a valid worldview is at the heart of this disdain, often combined with a lack of knowledge of the basis for this faith. As a former University teaching fellow in Church History, I have at times been startled at the pervasive Biblical illiteracy that is taken for granted in today's world. (One of my students even asked me once in class: "Is the book of Matthew in the New Testament?" Fortunately the other students in the class were courteous enough not

Preface

to react to what was an honest acknowledgement of ignorance.) While this incident represents something of an exceptional case, it does reflect a perception in the wider society that the Bible is irrelevant and the Christian message not worthy of intelligent study.

It is in this context that I raise the questions posed in this book. Underlying them all is the key issue: *Does Christianity have a sure foundation?* The chapter titles indicate the lines of enquiry that I will take in answering this question. I will firstly examine the extra-biblical evidence for Jesus, and then address the accounts of the Empty Tomb. From there, I will go on to explore the encounters with the Risen Lord which formed the basis of the early Christians' passionate message. The role of the Holy Spirit as the life-giving spirit of God, and as the empowerment for Christian life and witness is then discussed. The final chapter will discuss the role of miracles as witnesses to Christ in today's world.

It is my hope that this exploration will indicate that Jesus Christ is real, risen, and alive today, and that Christianity is, in fact, built upon sure foundations.

Acknowledgments

THE OFTEN-QUOTED PHRASE "No man is an island entire of itself; every man is a piece of the continent . . . "[1] is particularly true of this book. This interdependence goes deeper than mere assistance with the writing process; it also includes the people who have shaped—and continue to shape—the continent of my life, and who gave me the perspectives from which this book is written.

Firstly, my late mother, Jean Isobel Knowles (née Wishart), who brought me up in a knowledge of the Scriptures. These memorized Scriptures "came alive" when I was converted to Christ in 1960. Secondly, the late Pastor Ron Coady, who made the suggestion to me that I should learn Greek and Hebrew in order to deepen my understanding of the Scriptures. This ultimately led to my beginning theological study at the University of Otago in the 1980s.

At Otago, the late Professor Peter Matheson was a significant figure in my academic journey, first introducing me to the enthralling field of Church History, and then astonishing me by recommending that I undertake postgraduate study in the discipline. Peter became my mentor and doctoral supervisor, and I learned much from his historical and literary insights. Similarly, Professor Paul Trebilco, teacher, colleague, and friend, enlarged my understanding of the New Testament and its context in his courses in Biblical Studies.

1.. Donne, "Meditation XVII."

Acknowledgments

Specifically for this book, I record my thanks to Sr. Anne Enright, RSM, and to Robin Myles, who each read its manuscript and offered enthusiastic and encouraging comments.

And, most importantly, I thank Adrienne, my wife and life partner for fifty-one years. We have travelled the continent of life together, and learned and grown in Christ together. My love and thanks for your partnership and companionship on the journey.

Chapter 1

What is the evidence for Jesus?

DID JESUS EVER LIVE? This is an extreme question sometimes raised by opponents of Christianity. And if he *did* live, how embellished are the stories about him? Has the lily been gilded? What do we *really* know about Jesus for sure, apart from the Biblical account?

The answer to the last of these questions is "Surprisingly, quite a lot." Evidence for Jesus appears in a number of first- and early second-century non-Christian writings, as well as in the pages of the New Testament. When these accounts are compared, there is a large area of common ground that firmly anchors what is known about Jesus within the realm of historical certainty.

In this chapter, I will examine these non-Christian accounts, and consolidate them into a summary of what people in the first and second centuries knew about Jesus. Some of these data are attested by a number of these accounts; others by a single witness. This consolidation enables us to weigh the evidence to determine which data are more firmly established, and which are less so.

References to Jesus (and also to the Christian movement) are found in the writings of six first- and early second-century non-Christian authors. These are listed in chronological order below, and the direct references to Jesus are highlighted and enclosed in a box.

Sure Foundations

1. Josephus (writing about 93CE)

Flavius Josephus (37/38–after 100CE) was a Jewish historian. He had been involved in the Jewish War of 66–70CE and, after being taken to Rome as a prisoner, wrote his historical works there. He includes two references to Jesus in his *Antiquities of the Jews*. These are:

> a. Josephus, *Antiquities*, xviii.63–64 [scholars note that there is considerable Christian interpolation in this extract. These additions are placed in square brackets, and excluded from our consideration of the external evidence.]
>
> Now there was about this time Jesus, a wise man [if it be lawful to call him a man]; *for he was a doer of wonderful works, a teacher of such men as receive the truth with pleasure. He drew over to him both many of the Jews and many of the Gentiles.* [He was [the] Christ.] *And when Pilate, at the suggestion of the principal men amongst us, had condemned him to the cross, those that loved him at the first did not forsake him;* [for he appeared to them alive again the third day; as the divine prophets had foretold these and ten thousand other wonderful things concerning him.] *And the tribe of Christians, so named from him, are not extinct at this day* [i.e. 93CE].

Implications:

- Jesus was a "wise man."
- He did "wonderful works."
- He was a teacher of truth, and attracted a following among Jews and Gentiles.
- He was crucified on the order of Pilate (instigated by the leading Jews).
- His followers ("the tribe of Christians") continued until Josephus's time (93CE).

> b. Josephus, *Antiquities*, xx.9.1
> So he [the High Priest Ananus] assembled the Sanhedrin of judges, and brought before them the brother of *Jesus who was called Christ [or "the so-called Messiah"]*, whose name was James, and some others. And when he had formed an accusation against them as breakers of the law, he delivered them to be stoned.

Implications:

- Jesus was called Christ; and had a brother named James, who was executed by stoning.
- James was known as the brother of Jesus.
- Jesus was well-known, and recognized by some as the Messiah.

2. Pliny the Younger (writing about 112CE)

Plinius Caecilius Secundus C. (c.61–c.113CE; called Pliny the Younger to distinguish him from his uncle, Pliny the Elder, who had perished while observing the eruption of Vesuvius in 79CE), was a barrister and consul, who had received a special commission from the Emperor Trajan to govern the province of Bithynia in c.111CE. As governor, Pliny came across Christians who had been brought before his court on various charges, and, not having previously encountered them, is puzzled as to the appropriate legal precedent in dealing with them. He writes his letter to the Emperor seeking advice, and his description of the Christians' practices includes the following phrase:

> a. Pliny [the Younger], Book X, *Epistle* 96, written to Trajan
> It was their [the Christians'] habit on a fixed day to assemble before daylight and *recite by turns a form of words to Christ as a god* . . .

Implications:

- Christians gather to worship Christ as a god.
- The phrase "a form of words" suggests that a liturgy may have developed.

3. Tacitus (writing about 116CE)

P. Cornelius Tacitus (56–c.120CE) was a Roman historian, consul, and governor of the province of Asia under Trajan. His major historical works were the *Annals* (covering from 14 to 68CE) and the *Histories* (from 68CE onwards). The former work includes an extensive account of Christian persecution under Nero as scapegoats for the Great Fire of Rome in 64CE:

> a. Tacitus, *Annals*, XV.44:4
>
> *Christus,* from whom the name [Christians] had its origin, *suffered the extreme penalty during the reign of Tiberius at the hands of one of our procurators, Pontius Pilatus,* and a deadly superstition, thus checked for the moment, again broke out not only *in Judaea, the first source of the evil,* but also in the City [Rome] …

Implications:

- Christ was executed [crucifixion is not mentioned, but is implied as "the extreme penalty"] during the reign of Tiberius (i.e. 14–37CE).
- He was executed at the hands of Pontius Pilate, the Roman procurator in Judaea. [Pilate was procurator 26CE–36/37CE.]
- Jesus's influence continued after his crucifixion (the reference to a temporary setback implies that the "Jesus movement" had begun before his death).

4. Suetonius (writing about 120CE)

Suetonius Tranquillus C. (69–after 122CE) was, for a short time around 120CE, private secretary to the Emperor Hadrian. He wrote extensive biographical works, of which only his *Lives of the Caesars* and *On Famous Men* survive. In his *Life of Claudius* (part of his work on the *Lives of the Caesars*), he notes the expulsion of the Jews from Rome in c.49CE:

> a. Suetonius, *Life of Claudius*, xxv.4
> Since the Jews constantly made *disturbances at the instigation of Chrestus*, he expelled them from Rome....

Implications:

- This extract appears to refer to disturbances in the Jewish community, probably caused by the preaching of Christianity among them—hence, "disturbances at the instigation of Chrestus"—and is reflected in Acts 18:2, which refers to Aquila and Priscilla, who had recently arrived in Corinth "because Claudius had ordered all the Jews to leave Rome."

> b. Suetonius, *Life of Nero*, XVI.2
> Punishment was inflicted on *the Christians, a class of men given to a new and wicked [maleficus: magical] superstition.*

Implications:

- Christianity was seen as new, wicked, and superstitious.
- The inference of "magic" may relate to the accounts of healings and miracles accompanying the early Christians' evangelism.
- Suetonius does not connect this punishment with the Great Fire of Rome (64CE), for which Christians were made scapegoats, instead blaming Nero unequivocally for starting the fires.

5. Lucian of Samosata (writing about 165–70CE)

Lucian of Samosata (120–after 180CE) was a travelling lecturer and rhetorician, as well as an opponent of Christianity (which he saw as being pure charlatanry). His book *On the Death of Peregrinus* mocks Christian beliefs and practices, but in so doing makes observations which provide evidence for early Christianity:

> a. Lucian of Samosata, *Peregrinus* 11, 13
> (11)That other, . . . *whom they [Christians] still worship, the man who was crucified in Palestine because he introduced this new cult* into the world. (13) . . . worshipping that *crucified sophist* himself and living under his laws.

Implications:

- Jesus was crucified in Palestine
- He introduced a new cult (i.e. Christianity)
- Christians continue to worship Jesus

6. Mara bar Serapion (date of writing uncertain: after 73CE)

Little is known of Mara bar Serapion, but he was a Syriac Stoic writer (and not a Christian, although possibly having some awareness of Christianity). Although the dating is uncertain, he may have lived towards the end of the first century CE. He writes a letter from prison to his son, protesting his imprisonment by comparing it with the unjust suffering of "three wise men": Socrates, Pythagoras, and the "wise King" of the Jews (which appears to be a reference to Jesus):

> a. Mara bar Serapion, letter to his son
> What advantage did the Jews gain from *executing their wise King*? It was just after that that their kingdom was abolished [in 73CE]. . . . *Nor did the wise King die altogether; he lived on in the teaching he had given.*

Implications:

- Jesus was the wise "King of the Jews"
- Jesus was executed by the Jews
- Despite his death, Jesus's teaching continued to be influential

Consolidation of the data

So, to summarize the external evidence, what do we know about Jesus?

The strongest conclusion is that *Jesus was executed by crucifixion in Palestine at the order of Pontius Pilate during the reign of the Emperor Tiberius* (14–37CE). Four witnesses (Josephus, Tacitus, Lucian of Samosata, and Mara bar Serapion) all refer to his death (with two of these specifically stating that this was by crucifixion, and one inferring this fate by calling it "the extreme penalty"). Two of these witnesses (Josephus and Mara bar Serapion) also cite the antipathy of the Jewish authorities as an instigating factor in his execution. The first conclusion we therefore can draw from the external evidence is that Jesus was executed by crucifixion.

A second strong conclusion, also backed up by four witnesses, is that *Jesus's teaching and miracle-working ability had attracted a following among Jews and Gentiles, and that this following continued, and indeed expanded, after his death*. Josephus attributes this following to Jesus's wisdom, his wonderful works, and his teaching of truth. Josephus also records that the "tribe of Christians" continued to this day (i.e. 93CE); and Mara bar Serapion asserts that Jesus lived on in the teaching he had given. Tacitus's assessment is more negative (as would be expected from a Roman governor), referring to this continuing influence as a "deadly superstition" which was only temporarily checked by Jesus's death, and which was now beginning to expand beyond Judaea and to gain followers in the city of Rome itself. Finally, Lucian of Samosata makes the comment that Jesus had introduced a new cult into the world and that his followers continued "living under his laws." The external evidence therefore attests to the impact of Jesus's teaching and ministry, and its continuing (and indeed, expanding) influence, even after his death.

A third conclusion that can be drawn from the external evidence relates to the *assessment of Jesus, both by Christians (as noted by the external writers), and by the external writers themselves*. Jesus is called by a number of titles in the literature. Both Josephus and Mara bar Serapion refer to Jesus as "wise," with the latter author adding a further description of him as a "wise King" of the Jews. On a less positive note, Lucian of Samosata uses the term "sophist," which was originally a teacher of virtue, but later denoted a disparaging sense of one who uses clever and arbitrary reason in order to deceive. Lucian's negative assessment echoes that of Tacitus and Suetonius, who had earlier referred to Christianity as a deadly or magical superstition.

Conversely, Josephus recognizes that Jesus was acknowledged by some as the Messiah. His identification of James as "the brother of Jesus who was called Christ" is an indication that this Messianic claim was well-known. Two further witnesses (Pliny the Younger and Lucian of Samosata) also refer to the worship of Jesus. Lucian speaks of Christians worshipping "the man who was crucified in Palestine," and that they were "worshipping the crucified sophist himself," a clear reference to Jesus. Pliny is even more explicit, saying that "It was their [the Christians'] habit on a fixed day to assemble before daylight and recite by turns a form of words to Christ as a god. . . ." This indicates (1) that Christian worship took place on a particular day; (2) that a liturgy ("a form of words") may have developed for this worship; and (3) that this worship was offered "to Christ as a god."

Conclusion

The evidence of these non-Christian writers places the historicity of the Crucifixion beyond doubt. Indeed, it establishes the *event* of Jesus's death quite independently of the New Testament evidence. Even if the New Testament had never been written, we would still know from these writers that Jesus had been crucified at the orders of Pontius Pilate, i.e., that this was a *bona fide* historical event, independent of any faith-based claim. Similarly, these writers' evidence indicates that Jesus had attracted a following through his teaching and "wonderful works," and that this following continued (and indeed expanded) after his death. There is therefore continuity between the life and death of Jesus and the faith community that continued after him. These two factors (the crucifixion of Jesus and the persistence of a movement that adhered to his teachings) can therefore be regarded as firm historical foundations for Christianity.

Nevertheless, there are also elements of interpretation to be considered here. All history involves both the event under investigation and the historical interpretations placed upon it. Thus, while there might be a single acknowledged event, there may be a multiplicity of possible interpretations. We see this in the writings that we are addressing. While there are positive explanations of the life and death of Jesus (as recorded by these writers), there are negative ones also. Thus Jesus is called "a wise man," a teacher of truth, and a miracle-worker (Josephus); he is also called a "wise King" (Mara bar Serapion) and "the so-called Messiah" (Josephus), and worshipped as a god (Pliny the Younger). Negative interpretations of Jesus and his followers include: an "evil," a "deadly superstition", and a "new and wicked superstition" (Suetonius and Tacitus), a source of social conflict (Suetonius), and "a new cult" (Lucian of Samosata). Then, as now, opinions about Jesus were mixed.

Given such a variety, this leads to the important question of why Jesus's followers should have attributed significance to his death. What has led them to interpret his crucifixion as a salvific event, and not only to continue following his teachings, but also (as Pliny attests) to "worship him as a god"? What has created this perspective on the event and the interpretations that have been placed upon it? These questions will be discussed in greater detail in the next two chapters.

Chapter 2

The Resurrection and the Empty Tomb

IT HAS BEEN OBSERVED that history is inherently untidy and that it seldom moves in straight lines. (For example, who could have predicted in 1979 that the Soviet invasion of Afghanistan under Leonid Brezhnev that year would later lead to the fall of the Berlin Wall and the collapse of Communism, the rise of al-Qaeda and the 9/11 terrorist attack on the New York World Trade Centre, and the subsequent Second Iraq War of 2003–11?) Christianity is no exception to this susceptibility to change, having a number of "inflection points" in its historical trajectory. In mathematics, the term "inflection point" denotes a point on a curve where its curvature changes, e.g. from concave to convex. Its usage has expanded to refer to significant points at which an idea, or a set of ideas, changes. This application is possible because ideas are not fixed; they mutate—often through the integration of transforming insights—leading to changed perceptions and expectations.

Three such transformations have taken place in early Christianity: the Resurrection of Jesus; the reorientation of the church from its Jewish roots to a Gentile ethos later in the first century; and—a subsequent story—the "Constantinian Revolution" of the fourth century, when Christianity was no longer persecuted, but came to be favored and supported by the Roman State. Of these, the most important transformative event was the Resurrection of

Jesus. As John C. Lennox, Emeritus Professor of Mathematics at Oxford University, puts it: "[I regard] the resurrection of Christ ... as the supreme evidence for the truth of the Christian worldview.... It was the miracle of the resurrection of Christ that started Christianity going, and that same miracle is its central message."[1] The Resurrection therefore lies at the heart of Christianity: it changed the way that Jesus's disciples understood his message, and produced an all-encompassing change of worldview that would lead them to radical new understandings of who he was, what his teaching meant, and the ways in which his death was significant.

All of the disciples' preaching was based on the message that Jesus was alive and that he had conquered death. This dependence was admitted by the Apostle Paul: " ... if Christ has not been raised, our preaching is useless and so is your faith" (1 Cor.15:14). The Resurrection is therefore foundational to Christianity. But, by contrast to the Crucifixion of Jesus (which, as we have seen, is attested by several external witnesses), our evidence for this is derived from the accounts in the New Testament, and therefore reflects subjective "insider" perspectives. Let us begin by examining the context out of which these perspectives emerged.

The Context of the Resurrection

As both Mara bar Serapion and Lucian of Samosata have noted, Jesus's followers continued to follow his teaching and to live by his laws, even after his execution. Why did they persist in doing so? After all, his crucifixion had ended their hope that he was the Messiah. As the two disillusioned disciples on the Emmaus road acknowledged, " ... they crucified him; but we had hoped that he was the one who was going to redeem Israel. And what is more, it is the third day since all this took place" (Luke 24:20–21).This despondency was pervasive: when the disciples gathered together later that evening, they did so "with the doors locked for fear of the Jews" (John 20:19).

1. Lennox, *God and Stephen Hawking*, 83.

However, on reading accounts of past events, one must be aware of one's retrospective viewpoint; after all, we know how the story turned out. . . . *But importantly, the disciples did not!* It is easy for us to minimize their discouragement and fear, offering the mental equivalent of "there, there—it's going to be all right!" What was the situation as they saw it at that time? Their Leader had been crucified, ending their hopes of the Messianic kingdom that they had expected him to inaugurate. What is more, there would have been a profound sense of personal failure. They all had forsaken him and fled at his arrest at the Garden of Gethsemane (Matt.26:56; Mark 14:50); and although Peter, one of their leading disciples, had followed Jesus (at a distance) into the high priest's judgement hall, he had, on three occasions, denied that he was one of Jesus's followers, or even that he knew him (Matt.26:69–75; Mark 14:66–72; Luke 22:62–71; John 18:15–18, 25–27). The dejection of the two disciples on the Emmaus Road reflected the discouragement of the main body of disciples in Jerusalem.

This sense of despair comes out in—and was exacerbated by—events earlier that day, when Jesus's body had been reported as having gone missing from the tomb in which he had been laid after his crucifixion. The Empty Tomb has become an emblem for the Christian faith, a symbol of the Resurrection of Jesus. It is important to remember that *it was not seen as such on that first morning.* Rather, the absence of the body of Jesus led to fear, bewilderment, and puzzlement; the disciples were not predisposed to believe in the Resurrection. Indeed, the first reports of the Empty Tomb were met with unbelief and incredulity (Mark 16:11; Luke 24:11), and they took some convincing that Jesus had, in fact, risen from the dead. Why were the disciples not persuaded by these accounts? What were the "inflection points" that changed their minds, convincing them that Jesus had risen from the dead?

The Empty Tomb

All four Gospels offer accounts of the Empty Tomb. Some details vary, depending on the perspectives of the people involved. These

The Resurrection and the Empty Tomb

variations are entirely consistent with the nature of their stories as oral testimony. A general principle in dealing with oral accounts such as these is that differences in perspectives and viewpoints indicate a plurality of witnesses, and these multiple attestations imply greater reliability and authenticity. Conversely, a uniform set of accounts infers either a single source, or the possibility of collusion, and hence suggests a less reliable source of evidence.

The Gospels record eight witnesses at the Empty Tomb. These are:

- Mary Magdalene (Matt.28:1; Mark 16:1, 9; Luke 24:10; John 20:1)
- Mary, the mother of James (Mark 16:1; Luke 24:10)
- Salome (Mark 16:1)
- The other Mary (= Mary, the mother of James?) (Matt.28:1)
- Joanna (Luke 24:10)
- Other (unnamed) women (= "the others") (Luke 24:10)
- Simon Peter (Luke 24:12; John 20:3-6)
- The other disciple (= John) (John 20:8)

The first six occurrences all involve the testimony of a group of women; after hearing their story, Simon Peter and the other disciple go to the Empty Tomb to "check out" what had happened (i.e. a male validation of the women's story). This was because women's testimonies in the Roman world customarily carried little weight without the corroboration of males. This forms part of what Biblical scholars call a "criterion of embarrassment": i.e., if the Gospel accounts *had* been fabricated, then the Empty Tomb narrative would have been strengthened by making the male disciples the first to visit it and to ascertain that it was empty. The placing of the women as the first witnesses of the Empty Tomb is an "embarrassment," indicating that the Gospel writers are recording *what actually happened*, rather than what society would have expected to have happened. The role of the male witnesses has not been emphasized, indicating that the story has not been "embroidered" to conform to societal expectations, and that it accurately reflects the reality of what took place at the Empty Tomb.

1. What were the responses of the witnesses to the Empty Tomb?

An examination of the responses to the Empty Tomb reveals that these were predominantly negative. The women are variously described as "afraid" (Matt.28:5, 8; Mark 16:8); "alarmed" (Mark 16:5); "trembling and bewildered" (Mark 16:8); "wondering" (Luke 24:4); "frightened" (Luke 24:5); and as grieving and crying (John 20:10-11). Similarly, Peter is described as "wondering to himself what had happened" (Luke 24:12); and the disciples as not believing the women's testimony (Mark 16:11; Luke 24:11). Only "the other disciple" (i.e. John) is recorded as seeing and believing, although not understanding what had happened (John 20:8-9). Ironically, the only people who *are* recorded as believing the account of the Empty Tomb implicitly were the chief priests and the elders, who accepted that it was indeed empty, and devised a "cover story" that the disciples had stolen the body (Matt.28:11-15); this was exactly what they had feared would happen (Matt.27:62-66)!

The conclusion that one must draw is that *the Empty Tomb did not (by itself) lead to faith*! It was not enough to say that the Tomb was empty, since other explanations (i.e. theft of the body, either by the disciples, or by someone else) might explain what had happened. There is no doubt that Jesus's body had been in the Tomb, since Joseph of Arimathea and Nicodemus had placed it there, and rolled a stone in front of the Tomb (Matt.27:57-60; Mark 15:42-46; Luke 23:50-53; John 19:38-42). This was witnessed by Mary Magdalene and the other women who had followed Jesus (Matt.27:61; Mark 15:47; Luke 23:55-56). Furthermore, the Tomb was sealed and guarded at the express command of Pilate the following day (Matt.27:62-66). Given the delay, the guards would no doubt have checked that the body of Jesus was actually in the Tomb before placing the seal on the stone, and they were standing on duty at the moment of the Resurrection. Because the body had

The Resurrection and the Empty Tomb

disappeared, they were in danger of punishment for dereliction of duty (Matt.28:11-15).

2. Why are there no references to the Empty Tomb outside the Gospels?

It is noteworthy that the Tomb of Jesus is mentioned only once in the remainder of the New Testament: Paul refers to it in his sermon in Pisidian Antioch during his first missionary journey (Acts 13:29-31). Although he does not state specifically here that the Tomb is empty (v.29), this verse is immediately followed by the emphatic statements: "But God raised him from the dead" (v.30), and "for many days he was seen by those who had travelled with him from Galilee to Jerusalem" (v.31). Surprisingly, the Empty Tomb does not feature in Paul's summary of the Resurrection appearances in 1 Cor.15:3-8; scholars have surmised from this that Paul does not seem to know about it. Nor does he include the accounts of Mary Magdalene and the other women at the Tomb in his list. However, a reason for these exclusions may lie in the particular circumstances of Paul's relationship with the Corinthian church (a large subject in its own right). In the previous chapter, he has placed severe limits on the public role of women (1 Cor.14:34-35). This was a local restriction quite at variance with his practice in other churches, where his rule was "There is neither . . . male nor female, for you are all one in Christ Jesus" (Gal.3:28); the inclusion of eight female names in his list of coworkers in Rom.16 indicates his praxis elsewhere. A reference to women as the witnesses of the Empty Tomb would undermine the impact of his restriction on the Corinthian women.

Nor is the Tomb mentioned in Patristic literature until Eusebius of Caesarea, writing in 335CE, recorded that it had been buried under a mound of earth as part of a building programme initiated by the Emperor Hadrian. This followed his decision to build a Roman colony on the ruins of Jerusalem after the end of the Bar Kokhba Revolt of 132-35CE. Although a shrine of Venus was erected over the Tomb, Christians remembered where the sites—which included both Golgotha and the Tomb, only a few metres apart—had been, and when imperial persecution finally ended in 313CE, they petitioned the co-Emperor Licinius to have the earthworks removed and access restored. This took place in 326CE, after Constantine had become sole Emperor. Constantine ordered the Church of the Holy Sepulchre to be built on the site, encompassing both Golgotha and the Tomb within an overarching basilican complex.[2] Constantine's purpose in doing so was to create a place of pilgrimage, thus fostering religious—and hence imperial—unity within the Empire. More significance appears to have been placed on the site of Golgotha than on the Tomb, although Constantine ordered the removal of a rocky outcrop over the Tomb to enable easier access to it. This was completed in 335CE.

3. Does the Empty Tomb have limitations as evidence of Jesus's resurrection?

Part of the reason for the lack of focus on the Empty Tomb appears to lie in its evidential limitations. Firstly, it had geographical inadequacies. The Tomb reflected a local event, and would have been less significant for people outside of Jerusalem, who may not have been able to visit it for themselves. This lack of interest continued until the advent of pilgrimages in the fourth century. These were promoted particularly by Constantine's mother Helena, who had made a pilgrimage to the Holy Land in 326CE, and who was credited with the finding of the True Cross at Golgotha (although this discovery appears to be a later attribution). Her example fostered a new emphasis on pilgrimage, which restored the geographical sense of "holy places"; however, this appears to have focused more on Golgotha than on the Tomb.

A second evidential limitation was an historical one. As time passed, the Empty Tomb increasingly became the memory of an event in the past, and therefore of declining relevance in the

---

2. For a detailed illustrated account of this building project, see Telfer, "Martyry," 43–63.

present. This trend would have been compounded by the spread of the gospel into the Gentile world, in that the events surrounding the Empty Tomb were more distant, both in space and in time. There were also issues of transmission: if only those people who had been at the Empty Tomb could be authoritative witnesses of the resurrection, then their numbers would diminish as the original witnesses began to die. Geographically- and temporally-anchored "evidence" would become less sustainable as the Christian movement grew and evolved. By contrast, the disciples' transcendent encounters with the Risen Lord had no such limitation: they could happen *anywhere, at any time,* and *to anyone.* These encounters will be discussed in the next chapter.

4. Was the Resurrection expected?

A final issue concerns expectations of the Resurrection. If the early disciples had been anticipating it, then one might legitimately question whether their perceptions (and hence, their witness) were biased by this anticipation. However, what becomes clear from the New Testament accounts is that the Resurrection was both *unexpected* and *surprising.* There are several reasons for this.

Firstly, the disciples did not always understand what Jesus was telling them or the significance of his actions. For example, following his admonition to avoid the "yeast" (i.e. the teaching) of the Pharisees and of Herod, which the disciples interpreted as referring to their having forgotten to bring bread, he asked them "do you still not understand? . . . How is it you don't understand . . . ?" (Matt.16:9, 11). In another example, he called the disciples "dull" (Greek: *asunetoi,* "unable to put things together"), when they failed to understand his teaching on cleanness and uncleanness (Matt.15:16). Consequently, when Jesus several times explicitly predicted his crucifixion and resurrection, it is not surprising that his disciples did not understand what he was telling them, and were afraid to ask him about it (Mark 9:32; Luke 9:45).

Secondly, the placing of the first of these predictions immediately following Peter's confession of Jesus as the Christ (i.e.

the Messiah) (Matt.16:13–20; Mark 8:27–30; Luke 9:18–21) is an indication that Jesus did not fit Jewish understandings of the Messiah as a Davidic king who would sweep the Roman armies into the sea.[3] His predictions of his suffering, death, and resurrection were quite at variance with what was expected, leading Peter to take strong exception to what he had said (Matt.16:21–23).

Thirdly, while the belief in the Resurrection was based on the Old Testament (Job 19:25–26; Dan.12:2) and was held by most Jewish schools of thought (the exception being the Sadducees), this was seen as taking place on the Day of the Lord, when *all* the dead would be raised. Jesus's resurrection would not have been expected, since it was at odds with these Jewish understandings. What was at issue was his resurrection as *a single, present-day individual*, rather than as part of the whole body of deceased persons at the eschatological End. Thus, when Jesus told Peter, James, and John not to tell anyone what they had seen at the Mount of Transfiguration until after he was risen from the dead, "they kept the matter to themselves, discussing what 'rising from the dead' meant" (Mark 9:9–10).

Consequently, the unexpected and surprising nature of Jesus's Resurrection meant that even the disciples' initial encounters with the Risen Lord did not result in instant belief. Mary Magdalene failed to recognize him at first (John 20:10–16) and the two disciples on the Emmaus Road only recognized him in the evening as he broke bread with them, despite their having spent the afternoon walking with him and discussing the Scriptures (Luke 24:30–31). The classic example of this reluctance to believe is, of course, Thomas, who disbelieves the testimony of the other disciples and insists on seeing the Risen Lord for himself (John 20:24–29).

What does this hesitancy to believe say to us in the twenty-first century? From our postmodern perspectives, we might be inclined to criticize their first-century gullibility in accepting that Jesus had risen from the dead. However, what the New Testament record shows is that the Resurrection of Jesus went against their first-century expectations as well, and that they also required proof

3. Stanton, *Gospels and Jesus*, 242–43.

that it was real. Their encounters with the Risen Lord were just as revolutionary to them, as they would have been to our scientific, proof-seeking generation.

Conclusion

The Empty Tomb is a necessary component in the account of the Resurrection. However, it did not (*by itself*) lead to faith, and there are no references to it outside the Gospels. The unexpectedness of the resurrection also contributed to the disciples' lack of belief, and even their first encounters with the Risen Lord were hesitant and uncertain. So, given their initial reluctance to believe, what "proofs" brought the disciples to the joyful recognition that Jesus had risen indeed? How did the Resurrection bring about an all-encompassing change of worldview, leading to transforming new insights into who Jesus was, what his teaching meant, and the ways in which his death was significant? Because, make no mistake, this was *the* key inflection point for Christianity—the Resurrection changes everything!

Chapter 3

Encounters with the Risen Jesus

As has previously been noted, the Resurrection of Jesus is foundational for Christianity. It changed the way that Jesus's disciples understood who he was, what his teaching meant, and why his death was significant. But this transformation was not merely a change of thinking; their encounters with the Risen Jesus also led them into their own experience of the power of his Resurrection. This seems to have taken place in four stages:

- Stage 1: Seeing, but not recognizing
- Stage 2: Joyful recognition and believing
- Stage:3: Instruction and illumination
- Stage 4: Empowerment and dynamism

Stages 1 to 3 will be discussed in this chapter; Stage 4 will be dealt with in the next chapter.

Stage 1: Seeing, but not recognizing

Christianity can be characterized as an *experiential* faith. It had begun in the first disciples' experience of Jesus, starting with his call to "Come, follow me," and their immediate leaving of their nets to do so (Mark 1:17). As they followed him over the next three years, seeing his miracles and hearing his teaching, their recognition of who he was grew, culminating in Peter's pivotal confession: "You are the Christ, the Son of the living God" (Matt.16:16; Mark 8:29; Luke 9:20). Their experience made them very familiar with Jesus as a person. So, given this long association, why was he not immediately recognized in two of the initial post-Resurrection encounters (Mary Magdalene and the disciples on the Emmaus road)? While some of this could be attributed to the unexpected nature of the Resurrection, there is also the wider issue of recognizing the familiar in an unfamiliar context. Research by the School of Psychology at Keele University in 2021 has demonstrated the role of context in recognition. Using a surprise lecturer identification test across two experiments, the researchers found that "few students recognised their lecturer when they were unexpected, but accuracy was higher when the lecturer was preceded by a prompt." Their findings suggested that "familiar face recognition can be poor in unexpected contexts."[1]

This research finding applies to both Mary Magdalene's encounter and that of the disciples on the road to Emmaus. Mary was consumed by grief at the Tomb, and failed to recognize the Risen Jesus until he provided the "prompt" of calling her name (John 20:16). Similarly, the two disciples did not recognize him, since they knew that he was dead (Luke 24:13–21), and did not expect to see him in the unfamiliar context of the Emmaus road. Jesus's breaking of the bread at the evening supper provided the "prompt" of the familiar, since they would have seen him do exactly this at the feeding of the Five Thousand (Luke 9:16) and at the Last Supper (Luke 22:19). This led them to their recognition of him as Risen Lord (Luke 24:30–31).

Stage 2: Joyful recognition and believing

Other encounters on that first day include an appearance to Peter (noted in Luke 24:34 and 1 Cor.15:5), and to the Eleven disciples

---

[1]. Laurence et al., "Recognising Familiar Faces," 174–77, Abstract.

and the others gathered with them in the Upper Room (Mark 16:14–18; Luke 24:33–49; John 20:19–25). This encounter is the disciples' first collective engagement with the Risen Lord, and it sets the pattern for further post-Resurrection appearances over the next forty days (Acts 1:3–9). The Gospel writers treat the Upper-Room stories in a range of ways, with Luke and John providing the fullest accounts. While there are variations of emphasis, some common patterns can be discerned.

1. Jesus's appearances to his disciples

These took place in several different ways. The two appearances in the Upper Room are abrupt and startling (Mark 16:14; Luke 24:36; John 20:19, 26). Although the doors were locked for fear of the Jews (John 20:19), Jesus suddenly appears in the midst of the disciples gathered there. It is not surprising that they were initially startled and frightened, Luke observing that they thought they had seen a ghost (Luke 24:37). Although John does not directly refer to this frightened response, instead saying that the disciples were overjoyed when they saw the Lord, there may be an element of ironic humor in his account, in that Jesus greets the disciples twice (John 20:19, 21). "Peace be with you" (*shalôm 'alêchem*) is the equivalent of our colloquial "Gidday!" One can easily imagine the disciples as being so panicked by his sudden appearance and his first greeting that Jesus has to begin again.

Conversely, the Emmaus road encounter seems much more casual (Luke 24:14–16), with Jesus approaching the two disciples as they walked along the road and engaging in conversation with them. The crucial revelation of who he is does not occur until later in the story, when he breaks bread at the supper table in the evening (vv.30–31). This informality is also reflected in the later engagement at the Sea of Galilee, where Jesus calls the disciples to breakfast after their unsuccessful nightlong fishing expedition (John 21:4–14). Similarly, the references to his appearances over a forty-day period following the Resurrection seem almost nonchalant (Acts 1:3).

2. Proofs of the Resurrection

Jesus alleviates the fears of the disciples by offering them physical proofs of his Resurrection. In Luke, he asks them why they were troubled and doubtful, and offers them his hands and feet (still bearing the scars of the Crucifixion) to prove that he was a real, physical, body (Luke 24:37–40). He follows this up by asking for something to eat to demonstrate that he was not a disembodied spirit (Luke 24:41–43). John does not allude to any physical proofs in the first Upper Room encounter, but expands the bodily demonstration when Thomas (who had not been present) questions the testimony of the other disciples, and demands hard evidence. When Jesus reappears a week later, he invites Thomas to put his finger into the wounds in his hands and into the wound in his side. Thomas does so, and is convinced that Jesus is really risen (John 20:24–28). John's Gospel also indicates that Jesus offers other proofs of his resurrection, but does not identify these (John 20:30–31; 21:25). This implies that it tells only part of the story, selecting from a range of Jesus's known signs and miracles. Similarly, Acts states that Jesus "gave many convincing proofs that he was alive" (Acts 1:3), but does not give any further details. Nevertheless, the Greek word for "convincing proofs" (*tekmerion*: "that for which something is surely and plainly known, an indubitable evidence, a proof") indicates that such proofs were decisive for the apostles' faith.

3. The Response of the Disciples

By contrast to the Empty Tomb, which did not provide compelling evidence of the Resurrection, the encounters with the Risen Jesus were "inflection points" for the disciples' faith. They had seen their Master die on the Cross (and his hands and feet still bore the wounds to evidence this); now they had seen, heard, and touched him, and had been convinced that he was alive. Hence the account refers to their "joy and amazement" (Luke 24:41), and to being "overjoyed when they saw the Lord" (John 20:20). This is mirrored by the disciples on the Emmaus Road, whose hearts burned within them as Jesus talked with them on the road (Luke 24:32), as well as by the disciples in Jerusalem, who had their own exuberant report: "It is true! The Lord has risen and has appeared to Simon." (Luke 24:34)

But this joy was only the beginning. There are hints of more to come in the Upper Room story, and these would play out over the forty days leading up to Jesus's ascension. The first of these is a radical new understanding of the Scriptures (Luke 24:44–48, especially v.45); this will be explored under Stage 3: Instruction and illumination. The second anticipatory hint is contained in the references to the promise of the Holy Spirit. In all three accounts (Luke 24, John 20, and Acts 1), this empowerment by the Holy Spirit is linked to the commissioning of the disciples as Jesus's witnesses. This will be explored further under Stage 4: Empowerment and dynamism.

Stage 3: Instruction and illumination

The appearances of the Risen Lord were paralleled by instruction and illumination. It will be recalled that, during his ministry, the disciples had not always understood what Jesus was telling them, and even explicit references to his rising from the dead (Mark 9:9–10) were met with bewilderment. It is therefore not surprising that Jesus's death and resurrection produced massive crises of faith in the disciples—what had happened to him did not fit what they had expected. What did the Kingdom of God (the focus of Jesus's teaching) mean in the light of his crucifixion as the King of the Jews? How did these events fit into their understanding of what the Old Testament scriptures had predicted of the Messiah? And how did the Resurrection relate to their prior perceptions of who Jesus was and what he was doing?

These questions lie at the heart of the discussions of the two disciples on the Emmaus Road. Their statements about Jesus clearly indicate their Messianic expectations: "Jesus of Nazareth . . . was a prophet, powerful in word and deed before God and all the people. . . . They crucified him; but we had hoped that he was the one who was going to redeem Israel." (Luke 24:19–21) The Greek word translated "we had hoped" (ēlpizomen) is in the imperfect tense, indicating a past action or state which still continued. Their hope was not entirely extinguished, although three days had passed since his burial, and their discouragement and confusion are evident.

Jesus's response begins with a rebuke for their failure to believe all that the prophets had spoken. This shifted their focus away from their disappointment on to the Old Testament scriptures; his question "did not the Christ have to suffer these things and then enter his glory?" (Luke 24:26) then turned their Messianic understanding on its head. The Messiah was not the triumphant conqueror that they had expected, but instead a "suffering servant" who had been prophesied in the Scriptures. Jesus's death, which he had predicted immediately after Peter's confession of him as the Messiah (Matt.16:21), was in fulfilment of these prophecies; the crucifixion was not an aberration, or an abrogation of the Divine plan, but part and parcel of what the prophets had predicted. Jesus goes on to explain what all the scriptures, beginning with Moses and the prophets, had said about him (Luke 24:27).

However, the real illumination comes when Jesus broke bread at supper, when "their eyes were opened and they recognized him" (Luke 24:31). This recognition, together with the instruction that he had given on the road, produces a radical new understanding:

- Yes, Jesus had been crucified
- *But* his sufferings had been predicted in the Scriptures
- And now he had risen from the dead!

This was the key "inflexion point," the transforming insight, which changed all their perceptions and expectations. It is therefore not surprising that the two disciples at Emmaus exclaimed "Were not our hearts burning within us, while he talked with us on the road and opened the Scriptures to us?" and rushed back to Jerusalem to share the good news (Luke 24:32–33).

This process of instruction and illumination characterized other Resurrection encounters also. When Jesus appeared to the Eleven and their companions later that evening, he demonstrated the physical reality of his Resurrection and explained to them that everything that was written about him in the Law, the Prophets, and the Psalms had been fulfilled (Luke 24:44). Luke records that he then "opened their minds so they could understand the Scriptures," i.e. he showed them how the Old Testament had predicted his sufferings and rising from the dead on the third day, thus providing a new integrative framework for their understanding (Luke 24:45). This process of post-Resurrection reinterpretation and reorientation continued for forty days. Acts 1 records that Jesus carried on teaching until the day that he was taken up to heaven, giving instructions to the apostles, and speaking about the Kingdom of God (Acts 1:1-3). Although no details of this instruction are given, it evidently laid the foundation for the teaching of the apostles (Acts 2:42; 4:33) and for the emergence of the Christian traditions about the Resurrection (1 Cor.15:3-8).

Stage 4: Empowerment and dynamism

The encounters at Jesus's Resurrection were not only transformative events which changed the disciples' understanding of the Scriptures; they also introduced them to a power that they had never before experienced. One of the features of the Resurrection accounts is an emphasis on the empowerment of the Holy Spirit (Luke 24:48-49; Acts 1:2, 4-5, 8; John 20:22-23). This is most clearly stated in Luke, and especially in Acts, which is characterized by the dynamism that comes from the disciples' experience of the Spirit (Acts 2:42-47; 4:32-35). The role of the Holy Spirit, both in the Resurrection of Jesus and in the empowerment of the disciples, is a large and important subject, and we will therefore explore it in the following chapter.

Chapter 4

The Role of the Holy Spirit

Stage 4: Empowerment and dynamism

ALTHOUGH THE HOLY SPIRIT is referred to in the four Gospels, he is especially prominent in Acts. Stanton has observed that "it has very properly been suggested that Luke's second volume would be better entitled 'The Acts of the Holy Spirit'"[1] rather than the Acts of the Apostles. In this chapter, we will explore the role of the Holy Spirit in the Resurrection, and in the empowerment of the disciples, under four headings:

- The Holy Spirit and the vindication of Jesus
- The Holy Spirit as the life-giving active agent in the Resurrection
- The Holy Spirit and the Great Commission
- The Holy Spirit and the empowerment to witness

1. The Holy Spirit and the vindication of Jesus

The Holy Spirit plays an authenticating role in Jesus's ministry as the Messiah. At his baptism by John, the Holy Spirit descends on

---

1. Stanton, *Gospels and Jesus*, 87.

him like a dove, accompanied by a voice from heaven proclaiming him as the Son of God (Matt.3:16–17 *"This [one] is my Son . . . "*). Similarly, John the Baptist explicitly links Jesus's Messiahship to the Baptism of the Spirit (John 1:32–34); and Peter testifies that "God anointed Jesus of Nazareth with the Holy Spirit and power, and . . . he went around doing good and healing all who were under the power of the devil, because God was with him" (Acts 10:38). The Holy Spirit was the validating factor of Jesus's earthly ministry.

But this issue has further dimensions. An early doctrinal summary (1 Tim.3:16) refers to Jesus being "vindicated by the Spirit." What does this statement mean? The Greek word here translated "vindicated" is *edikaiōthē*, from the root *diakioō* (to justify, or to declare to be righteous). This is the same root word that Paul uses throughout Romans and Galatians to describe the believer's justification ("making or declaring right") by faith. Thus the person who was previously condemned ("in the wrong"), is now, by the unmerited grace of God, declared to be justified ("in the right"). The way in which this restored relationship with God could be attained lay at the heart of Martin Luther's concerns, and dominated the early stages of the Protestant Reformation. But this usage raises the question: how does this word apply to Jesus? What does it mean that he has been justified (vindicated or "declared to be right") by the Spirit? Recall that Jesus had been executed by the Romans as a condemned criminal. This raised massive questions about the legitimacy of his Messianic claims. As Paul rightly notes, his crucifixion was a stumbling block to the Jews and foolishness to the Greeks (1 Cor.1:23). Surely such a person could not be the chosen one of God; he must (at best) be sadly deluded, or (at worst) a liar? How can we know that he really was who he claimed to be?

These questions are answered through his vindication by the Spirit. This can be interpreted in two ways. It can be seen as a *completed* vindication, in terms of Jesus being raised from the dead by the Spirit. This Resurrection proved the truth of Jesus's assertions about himself, that he was truly the Messiah and that he had risen from the dead as he had said he would. However, it can also be seen in terms of an *ongoing* vindication by the coming of the Spirit.

Jesus had earlier promised to send the Spirit (John 14:26; 15:26; 16:7); the fulfillment of this promise on the Day of Pentecost was proof positive that he had been glorified (John 7:39) and that he was raised to be at the right hand of the Father (Acts 2:33). The activity of the Holy Spirit in the witness of the disciples was an ongoing vindication of Jesus as the Risen Lord.

Paul expands on the declaratory function of the Holy Spirit in Rom.1:3-4: "Regarding his Son, who as to his human nature was a descendent of David, and who through the Spirit of holiness was declared with power to be the Son of God by his resurrection from the dead, Jesus Christ our Lord." Not only was Jesus vindicated by the Holy Spirit in his Resurrection, he was also declared (*horizō*: "defined," "determined," "appointed") to be the Son of God through that same Spirit by the Resurrection. Thus Peter could say, in his explanatory sermon on the day of Pentecost, that "God has made this Jesus, whom you crucified, both Lord and Christ" (Acts 2:36). Not only was Jesus the Christ (i.e. the Messiah); he was also Lord. Consequently, as Paul declares in the Philippian hymn, "at the name of Jesus every knee should bow, in heaven and on earth and under the earth, and every tongue confess that Jesus Christ is Lord, to the glory of God the Father" (Phil.2:10-11).

2. The Holy Spirit as the life-giving active agent in the Resurrection

The Holy Spirit can be described as the life-giving active agent of God's purposes. The connection between the Spirit and the giving of life is implicit in both the Old and New Testaments, with the words *rûaḥ* (Hebrew) and *pneuma* (Greek) both connoting breath, wind, and spirit. The overlap between these triple meanings is most clearly seen in the "Dry Bones" vision of Ezek.37:1-10: "Come from the four *winds*, O *breath*, and breathe into these slain, that they may live" (v.9); the italicized words "winds" and "breath" are both translations of the same Hebrew word *rûaḥ*. The result of this gentle breeze is that these bones are activated to life. Similarly, Gen.1:2: "the Spirit of God [*rûaḥ 'Elōhîm*] was hovering [*mᵉraḥepeṯ*: brooding, fluttering tremulously] over the waters," incubating the creation of life.

This life-giving function of the Holy Spirit can be clearly seen in the Resurrection of Jesus. The word *zōopoieō* ("to cause to live, to make alive"), used of the Spirit several times in the New Testament (John 6:63; 1 Cor.15:45; 2 Cor. 3:6), is specifically applied to the Resurrection:

- Rom.8:11 And if the Spirit of him who raised Jesus from the dead is living in you, he who raised Christ from the dead will also *give life* to your mortal bodies through his Spirit who lives in you.

- 1 Pet.3:18 [Christ] was put to death in the body but *made alive* by the Spirit . . .

But there is more: the Holy Spirit is not only the life-giving agent of God in the Resurrection of Jesus; he is also the active agent of God giving life to our mortal bodies through his indwelling (Rom.8:11). This link between what the Holy Spirit *has done* in the Resurrection of Christ, and what he *continues to do* in the lives of Christians, permeates the New Testament, particularly in Paul's epistles. Paul insists that the believer is united with Christ's life by the Holy Spirit, and that Christians have been incorporated into Christ in his death, burial, and resurrection:

- Rom.6:3–6 Don't you know that all of us who were baptized into Christ Jesus were baptized into his death? We were therefore buried *with him* through baptism into death in order that, just as Christ was raised from the dead through the glory of the Father, we too may live a new life.

    If we have been united *with him* like this in his death, we will certainly also be united *with him* in his resurrection. For we know that our old self was crucified *with him* so that the body of sin might be done away with, that we should no longer be slaves to sin. . . .

- Eph.2:5-6 [God] made us alive *with Christ* even when we were dead in transgressions—it is by grace you have been saved. And God raised us up *with Christ* . . .

- Col.2:20; 3:1, 3 You died *with Christ* to the basic principles of this world. . . . You have been raised *with Christ*. . . . For you died and your life is now hidden *with Christ* in God.

- Gal.2:20 I have been crucified *with Christ* and I no longer live, but Christ lives in me. The life I [now] live in the body, I live by faith in the Son of God, who loved me and gave himself for me.

The highlighted words "*with Christ*"/"*with him*" illustrate Paul's insistence that Christians have been united with Christ in his death, burial, and resurrection. But Paul also emphasizes our incorporation into Christ's *life*. His reference to believers being "*in Christ*"/"*in him*" is a characteristic motif of his theology, appearing more than sixty times in his Epistles. Thus:

- Rom.8:1-2 There is now no condemnation for those who are *in Christ Jesus*, because through Christ Jesus the law of the Spirit of life set me free from the law of sin and death.

- 1 Cor.1:30 It is because of him [God] that you are *in Christ Jesus*, who has become for us wisdom from God—that is, our righteousness, holiness and redemption.

- 2 Cor.5:17 Therefore, if anyone is *in Christ*, he is a new creation; the old has gone, the new has come!

- Col.2:6-7 So then, just as you received Christ Jesus as Lord, continue to live *in him*, rooted and built up *in him*, strengthened in the faith as you were taught, and overflowing with thankfulness.

The Christian life is not a matter of trying to fulfil a set of legalistic "dos and don'ts," but rather of our being united *with Christ* and our living *in Christ*. The Holy Spirit is the active agent in this union: "if the Spirit of him who raised Jesus from the dead is living in you, he who raised Christ from the dead will also *give life* to your mortal bodies through his Spirit who lives in you" (Rom.8:11). Hence the statement in 1 Cor.1:30 that believers are *in Christ Jesus* because of God's action, and also that receiving Christ Jesus as Lord (Col.2:6) is the starting point of the Christian life. Believers are united with Christ, not merely in a theoretical sense, but through a real participation in the active life-giving Holy Spirit that had raised Christ from the dead.

How does one live out this Christian life? This is a product of living in the Spirit. Through Christ Jesus, the "law of the Spirit of life" sets us free from the "law of sin and death" (Rom.8:2), and enables us to live day by day by the enabling power of the Spirit. Being "filled with the Spirit" is to be filled with his life-giving, enabling power to live the kind of life to which we are called in Christ. It is not simply a matter of having spiritual gifts (although these are important), nor even of the "fruit of the Spirit" (Gal.5:22–23, note also v.25) but of letting the Holy Spirit work in and work out Christ's power (i.e. the gifts) and Christ's character (i.e. the fruits) in our life. He is the source; he is the life giver; he is the enabler.

It is in this sense that the Holy Spirit becomes not just a theoretical theological construct, but a present life-giving actuality in the lives of Christians. The Resurrection is not just the fact that Christ rose from the dead (by the power of the Spirit) at a point in the past, but that he is alive today and lives within the believers (by the power of the same Spirit). He has not only *risen*; he *lives today*!

3. The Holy Spirit and the Great Commission

The accounts of the Resurrection include a commission to be witnesses of the Risen Lord. The scope of this commission was global: to "all nations" (Matt.28:19; Luke 24:47), to "all creation" (Mark 16:15); and "to the ends of the earth" (Acts 1:8). Christianity therefore was born with a worldwide focus. This indicates the universal importance of the "Good News": if Jesus has indeed risen from the dead, this has implications for every person on the face of the earth.

The Role of the Holy Spirit

But what was a witness and what were these witnesses to preach? The cognate Greek words for "witness" (*martureō, marturia, marturion,* and *martus*) occur 171 times in the New Testament, and indicate "an affirmation that one has seen or heard or experienced something." As has previously been noted, Christianity is *experiential*, based on an encounter with Jesus Christ. The witnesses therefore are simply telling what they had seen, heard, and experienced: as Peter and John declared while on trial before the Sanhedrin, "We cannot help speaking about what we have *seen* and *heard*". (Acts 4:20) Similarly, 1 John begins with an emphatic declaration: "That which was from the beginning, which we have *heard*, which we have *seen* with our eyes, which we have *looked at* and our hands have *touched*—this we proclaim concerning the Word of life. . . . We have *seen* it and testify to it, and we proclaim to you the eternal life, which was with the Father and has appeared to us. We proclaim to you what we have *seen* and *heard* . . . " (1 John 1:1–3).

This uncompromising experiential witness is characteristic of the early chapters of Acts:

- Acts 2:32 God has raised this Jesus to life, and we are all *witnesses* of the fact.

- Acts 3:15 God raised him from the dead. We are *witnesses* of this.

- Acts 4:33 With great power the apostles continued to *testify* (*martureō*: witness) to the resurrection of the Lord Jesus . . .

- Acts 5:30–32 The God of our fathers raised Jesus from the dead. . . . We are *witnesses* of these things. . . .

- Acts 13:30–31 But God raised him from the dead, and for many days he was seen by those who had travelled with him from Galilee to Jerusalem. They are now his *witnesses* to our people.

The reference to "they [i.e. the apostles] are now his witnesses to our people" in Acts 13:31 might indicate that this witnessing role was a specialized one. (After all, the qualification for Judas's replacement as an apostle in Acts 1:21–22 included participation throughout the whole period of Jesus's ministry from his baptism by John through to his ascension, and especially, having been a witness of the resurrection.) However, Acts indicates that the role of witness extended considerably beyond the twelve apostles. Despite not being apostles, Stephen and Philip were powerful charismatic witnesses, and their preaching was accompanied by "great wonders and miraculous signs" (Acts 6:8; 8:5–7). Furthermore, when persecution broke out at the martyrdom of Stephen and the disciples were scattered, "those who had been scattered preached the word wherever they went" (Acts 8:4). This "scattering" specifically excluded the apostles, who remained behind in Jerusalem (Acts 8:1). (There is a note of irony here, in that the word "apostle" literally means "one who is sent"; everyone went out preaching, *except* the "sent ones"!) The fruitful "grassroots" witnessing of ordinary disciples such as these led to the extension of the gospel into the Gentile world. This can be seen most clearly in Acts 11:19–21, when those who had been scattered by Stephen's persecution evangelized in Phoenicia, Cyprus, and Antioch, and other disciples from Cyprus and Cyrene also began to tell the Antiochene Greeks the good news about the Lord Jesus, gaining many converts. The activities of these unknown, unnamed, witnesses exemplify the fervor with which the early Christians embraced the Great Commission.

It should be noted that this "grassroots" success in Antioch is followed up by continued input from the church in Jerusalem (Acts 11:22–30). This indicates a network; "witness" represents a community enterprise, as much as a purely individual one. The links between community and individual witness are demonstrated by New Testament scholar Richard Bauckham, who observes that a number of named characters appear in one or more Gospel narratives, although they take no active part in the story. He suggests that many of these named characters were *eyewitnesses* who not only originated the traditions to which their names are attached, but also continued to tell these stories as authoritative guarantors of their traditions as long as they lived. These people were well-known in their Christian communities, and the Gospel writers themselves may have known them. Bauckham's examples include Simon of Cyrene, who carried the cross for Jesus. Simon is identified in Mark as the father of Alexander and Rufus (Mark 15:21), but his sons are not named in the other Gospel parallels (Matt.27:32; Luke 23:26). Similarly, Bartimaeus is named in Mark (Mark 10:46), but not in the other Synoptic accounts of his healing (Matt.20:30; Luke 18:35). The naming of the women at the Empty Tomb is also varied: Mary Magdalene is named in all four accounts; Mark also includes Salome (Mark 16:1), while Luke includes Johanna (Luke 24:10). Neither of these two additional women is named in Matthew and John. Bauckham's thesis is that these names represent people who are known in the specific communities within which these Gospels were written. Those in the Markan community could refer to Alexander and Rufus for firsthand testimony about their father Simon's experience, or to Bartimaeus about his healing by Jesus, or to Salome about the Empty Tomb encounter. Similarly, the Lukan community could gain additional testimony about the Empty Tomb from Johanna. Bauckham therefore argues that there were numerous such grassroots "witnesses" available to authenticate the stories recorded in the Gospels. A wide range of sources therefore lay behind the Gospels, reinforcing the authoritative oral witness of the apostles.[2]

4. The Holy Spirit and the empowerment to witness

We have already noted the role of the Holy Spirit as the empowering agent in the Resurrection of Jesus and in the life of the Christian. Luke-Acts emphasizes this empowerment in terms of witness; other Gospels express the connection in different ways. In Matthew, the role of the Spirit is not stated, but the commission to "go and make disciples of all nations" is predicated on the Risen Lord's declaration: "All authority (*exousia*) in heaven and on earth has been given to me. Therefore, go . . ." (Matt.28:18–19). The word *exousia* means "liberty of action, authority, power, right,

---

2. Bauckham, *Jesus and the Eyewitnesses*, 39, 45, 47, and 51.

jurisdiction." A similar focus appears in the Johannine account of the Spirit, where Jesus commissions the disciples, breathing on them and saying "Receive the Holy Spirit. If you forgive anyone their sins, they are forgiven . . . " (John 20:22–23). This empowerment has resonances with Jesus's "keys of the kingdom" authorization following Peter's messianic declaration in Matt.16:19.

However, Luke-Acts—and, to a lesser extent, Mark—place a different focus on the empowerment of the Holy Spirit. The commission in Mark 16:15, "Go into all the world and preach the good news to all creation," is followed in vv.17–18 by a list of miraculous signs that would accompany those who believe. These include "they will speak with new tongues" (v.17), signalling that these signs are worked by the enabling of the Holy Spirit. The clearest indications of the link between the Holy Spirit and the empowerment to witness appear in Luke-Acts (Luke 24:48–49; Acts 1:8). Here Luke uses a different word (*dunamis*: power) to describe this empowerment. *Dunamis* means "strength, ability, power; inherent power, residing in a thing by virtue of its nature, or which a person or thing exerts or puts forth." It is a word that indicates action. The words *exousia* and *dunamis* are therefore related and complementary; the former indicating the right, or designated permission, to act (i.e. authority), and the latter, the inherent capability or miraculous power to perform an action (i.e. power, ability).

In the New Testament, this *dunamis* was often demonstrated in miracles. Thus "Stephen, a man full of God's grace and *power*, did great wonders and miraculous signs among the people" (Acts 6:8). Paul could remind his readers that "my message and my preaching were not with wise and persuasive words, but with a demonstration of the Spirit's *power*" (1 Cor.2:4), and that "our gospel came to you not simply with words, but also with *power*, with the Holy Spirit and with deep conviction" (1 Thess.1:5; compare 1 Cor.4:19–20). He later summarized his ministry as having been "by the *power* of signs and miracles, through the *power* of the Spirit of God. So from Jerusalem all the way around to Illyricum [modern-day Albania], I have fully proclaimed the gospel of Christ." (Rom.15:19) Paul's gospel was not only *preached*; it was also *demonstrated*.

The Role of the Holy Spirit

This spiritual power was pervasive and unrestricted: "grassroots" witnessing was paralleled by "grassroots" empowerment. Paul is very clear that the charismatic enabling of the Holy Spirit is available to every believer: "we were all baptized by one Spirit into one body—whether Jews or Greeks, slave or free—and we were all given the one Spirit to drink" (1 Cor.12:13). Because of this, the gifts of the Spirit are available to all members of the Body of Christ (1 Cor.12:4–11; 14:31), their various manifestations being unified by the same God who works all things in all (1 Cor.12:6). And, indeed, there *are* differences: in listing the gifts of the Spirit (vv.8–10), Paul notes that some gifts (e.g. word of wisdom, word of knowledge, healing, miracles, prophecy, discerning of spirits, and interpretation of tongues) are given to *alloi* (another, of the same kind), and other gifts (e.g. faith and tongues) are given to *heteroi* (another, of a different kind). Not all recipients of spiritual gifts are the same kind of people! Yet despite this diversity, "all of these [gifts] are the work of the one and the same Spirit, and he gives them to each one, just as he determines" (v.11). So while the charismatic enabling of the Spirit is available to every member of the Body of Christ, there are diversities of gifts, service, and working, but all by the same Spirit (vv.4–6).

Consequently, while there is a clear emphasis in Acts on the Holy Spirit working through the apostles (Acts 4:33; 5:12, etc.), other non-apostles, such as Stephen (Acts 6:5, 8) and Philip (Acts 8:5–8, 13) are also recorded as being filled with the Spirit and working miraculous signs. Saul's healing and being filled with the Spirit at the hands of Ananias (Acts 9:17–18) is another indication of the Holy Spirit working through ordinary believers. Paul can ask the Galatians: "Does God give you his Spirit and work miracles among you because you observe the law, or because you believe . . . ?" (Gal.3:5), demonstrating that the Galatians' believing provided them with access to the Holy Spirit and his miracle-working power. Furthermore, in his summary of appointed gifts in the Church at the end of 1 Cor.12, Paul makes a distinction between apostles and prophets, on the one hand, and the working of miracles and the gifts of healing, on the other: "In the church, God has appointed first of all apostles, second prophets, third teachers, then workers of miracles, also those having gifts of healing..." (1 Cor.12:28). All of these spiritual gifts and ministries are the work of the Holy Spirit in the Body of Christ, and "each one of you is a part of it" (v.27). The listing of miracles and healing separately from the apostles and prophets is an indication that these particular gifts were not limited to these leaders, but were available to all members of the Body of Christ enabled by the Holy Spirit.

These miraculous gifts continued up to the third century CE (and beyond). Irenaeus, writing about 180CE, states that:

> Those who are in truth his disciples ... do in his name perform [miracles] ... according to the gift which each one has received from Him. For some do certainly and truly drive out devils, so that those who have thus been cleansed from evil spirits frequently both believe [in Christ], and join themselves to the church.... Others still, heal the sick by laying their hands upon them, and they are made whole. Yea, moreover ... the dead even have been raised up, and remained among us for many years.... (Irenaeus, *Against Heresies*, ii, 32.4).

Origen (writing about 230CE) refers to Christians who, by the Holy Spirit "expel evil spirits, and perform many cures... according to the will of the Logos [i.e. the Word]" (Origen, *Against Celsus*, i.46). A later example is Antony of Egypt, founder of eremitic monasticism (i.e. monks living in solitude in the desert [*herēmos* = desert, hence the word "hermit"]), who is recorded as performing healings and exorcisms on his visit to Alexandria in 311CE: "through him the Lord healed the bodily ailments of many present, and cleansed others from evil spirits" (Athanasius, *Life of Antony*, xiv).

Conclusion

Three words capture the essence of the beginnings of Christianity: *experiential*, *enlightened*, and *empowered*. The encounters with the Risen Lord were transformative "inflection points" for the disciples' faith. They had seen him, heard him, and physically touched his resurrected body. They therefore knew *by experience* that he had risen, and could bear witness that he was indeed alive. But what did all this mean? The impact of these encounters was reinforced by *enlightenment*, as Jesus instructed them in new understandings of the Scriptures after his resurrection. This provided a new interpretative framework that formed the foundation of their post-Resurrection message. The final component was the *empowerment* of the Holy Spirit on the Day of Pentecost, which enabled them as Spirit-filled witnesses to show forth the reality of Jesus's resurrection. This empowerment was not confined to convincing preaching, but included the demonstration of the Holy Spirit's power in healings and miracles. Nor was this empowerment limited; the gifts of the Holy Spirit were available to all members of the Body of Christ. This powerful, Spirit-enabled, "grassroots" witness formed the beginnings of Christianity.

Chapter 5

That was then, this is now . . .

WHAT, THEN, SHALL WE say to these things? Church historian Jaroslav Pelikan has famously said that "if Christ is risen, nothing else matters. And if Christ is not risen—nothing else matters."[1] While this aphorism might seem to be a contradiction in terms, Pelikan meant by this that the resurrection is either the most significant event in history, an ultimate truth besides which everything else is secondary; or, if Christ is not risen, then the resurrection is illusory, the Christian faith is fallacious, and life has no meaning beyond this temporal world. However, the testimony of the early Christians was unequivocal: Christ is risen indeed, and his resurrection has cosmic significance. But the questions might then be asked: what relevance does a first-century event have in the twenty-first century? What can a past event say to us in our present and, indeed, in our future? After all, that was then, this is now. . . .

These questions are particularly apposite to the issue of miracles. The modern worldview is that although miracles happened in New Testament times, they no longer happen today. This viewpoint is rooted in the Enlightenment rationalism of the eighteenth century, exemplified by sceptic philosopher David Hume's *Essay on Miracles*, widely regarded as demonstrating their impossibility. But, as C.S. Lewis has pointed out in his seminal study of miracles,

---

1. Pelikan, cited in Arnold, "If Christ Is Risen, Nothing Else Matters."

Hume's denial is based upon a prior materialist/naturalist world view which explains the universe solely in terms of physical constants such as mass and energy. In this world view, all knowledge is empirical, based upon the evidence of the senses; Nature is all there is, and leaves no space for miracles to occur. Lewis convincingly refutes Hume's view, demonstrating the supernaturalist/theist world view of the universe as the creation of a supernatural, personal God, in which miracles can, and do, happen.[2] His argument has been utilized and extended by John Lennox, particularly in the context of his debates with Richard Dawkins, Christopher Hitchins, and other representatives of the "New Atheism."[3] This worldview is, of course, the Christian position, which is based upon the evidence of the supreme miracle: Jesus's resurrection. Because Jesus is risen from the dead, Christian faith has a sure, evidential foundation; and this reality is demonstrated by the power of the Holy Spirit.

But the Resurrection is not only an event in the past; Jesus is alive *today*. Encounters with the Risen Lord are not limited by circumstances of time or space (not even to being in a church!), but can happen *anywhere*, at *any time*, and to *anyone*. The active agent in an encounter with Christ is the Holy Spirit, who draws us to Christ and makes Christ real *to* us, *with* us, and *in* us. This is not merely an historical or theoretical belief, but is a living day by day reality in the lives of millions of Christians today. The channels of this encounter may vary: some receive Christ sacramentally, through participating in the Eucharist; others may experience him by illumination through the words of Scripture; still others might encounter him experientially by inviting him into their lives as Savior and Lord. Whatever the means by which Christ is encountered, the active life-giving agent is the Holy Spirit: *Christ is alive today and lives within believers by the power of the Holy Spirit.*

The agency of the Holy Spirit is also evident today in the empowering of Christian witness and mission. This is not necessarily

---

2. Lewis, *Miracles: A Preliminary Study*.

3. Lennox, *Miracles: Is Belief in the Supernatural Irrational?*; Lennox, *Gunning for God*.

a formal, organizational activity, but can take place in any context or circumstance, as "real people" tell their stories of what they have seen, heard, and experienced of Jesus. Christian witness is a *real* sharing of a *real* experience. And, just as in New Testament times, believers can expect the Holy Spirit to demonstrate the reality of their testimony by means of his supernatural power. It is to the credit of the twentieth-century Pentecostal and Charismatic movements that they have revived the experiential focus on the power of the Holy Spirit that had characterized the Early Church. Their openness to the miraculous may explain why these movements have grown exponentially in the last sixty years. Indeed, as a Pentecostal historian, I have often noted the role of healing movements as providing a constituency for the emergence of a Pentecostal movement or church (for examples, see Knowles, *New Life*; Knowles, *Transforming Pentecostalism*).[4] This is particularly the case in the Global South. Candy Gunther Brown notes that "divine healing practices are an essential marker of Pentecostal and Charismatic Christianity as a global phenomenon," and gives a striking example: "In the Latin American, Asian, and African countries where pentecostal growth is occurring most rapidly, as many as 80–90 percent of first-generation Christians attribute their conversions *primarily* to having received divine healing for themselves or a family member."[5]

I can give personal examples of this. My first experience of the living Jesus came at a healing campaign, conducted by American Pentecostal evangelist A.S. Worley, in my home town of Timaru, New Zealand, in June/July 1960. This five-week campaign was significant for some remarkable healings, including that of a young boy born with a club foot. This created much interest; so much so that the local *Timaru Herald* wrote up a three-column article on it two days later.[6] This newspaper report drew people from all

---

4. Knowles, *New Life*, 41–45, 51, and 58–64; Knowles, *Transforming Pentecostalism*, 17–24, 75–77.

5. Brown, "Introduction," 3. Emphasis Brown.

6. "Parents say Prayer Transformed Boy's Twisted Foot: Now Walks Unaided," *Timaru Herald*, 6 July 1960, 12, cited in Knowles, *New Life*, 59, footnote 17.

over the South Island to these meetings, and numerous other healings took place. As a result, some six hundred people (including the author) were converted to Christ during the campaign, many of whom have remained active Christians to the present day (for a fuller account, see Knowles, *New Life*. Extracts are given in the next two paragraphs.)[7]

However, while the miracles attracted public attention, the key characteristic of the campaign was the reality of the living Christ. This permeated the meetings, creating a sense of electric expectancy, exemplified in the fervent singing of the hymn "He lives, He lives, Christ Jesus lives today!"[8] The preaching was simple, straightforward, and positive, and was characterized by an emphasis on the person and ministry of Jesus. And, as people were invited to come to the front of the hall to receive Christ, "[t]he reaction of the congregation was extraordinary: it was quite common for complete strangers to get up from their seats and to come up and warmly shake the hands of the 'converts' returning to their seats. One of the early converts (Lilian Wright) remembers this as being one of the particular features of the campaign: 'you could *feel* the love of God in the meetings: the air was full of it.'"[9]

Following this, "a 'prayer line' was called for the sick, and these people came forward, and were individually prayed for by Brother Worley. The atmosphere was expectant and reverent: there was no sense of 'hype.' . . . Many people were healed: Lilian Wright, for example, told me that her husband had been healed of an arthritic back, and never had any trouble with it again."[10] Another eyewitness account of these healings is recorded by Mary Henderson:

> The fact that Jesus Christ is the same yesterday, today and forever is being confirmed on every hand.
>
> A little boy receives prayer for his eyes. Still wearing his glasses he asserts that 'the people look all funny.'

7. Knowles, *New Life*, 58–64.
8. A.H. Ackley, "He Lives!" cited in Knowles, *New Life*, 60, footnote 19.
9. Knowles, *New Life*, 60. Emphasis as cited.
10. Knowles, *New Life*, 60.

> The glasses are removed—he smiles. 'It's not funny now.' His glasses join the collection of discarded crutches and built-up shoes.
>
> A young man who has come up from Gore to the service, is healed of a back condition and throws his crutches away. Next day he is seen running up the street to catch a bus.
>
> A man looks down and watches the eczema disappear from the backs of his little boy's hands.
>
> A woman whose hands are twisted with arthritis sees her fingers uncurl and straighten out....[11]

Healings such as these pointed to the reality of the living Christ. After the end of the campaign, Worley summarized its impact: "Now you have tasted the good Word of God and have come in contact with the living Christ . . . you will never be satisfied with anything less than this you have tasted. . . . You can never be satisfied again with mere forms and ceremonies and Social Gospel. Only the living Christ with His miracles of healing and the fellowship of born-again believers will ever bring true joy and satisfaction to your hearts."[12] The reality of the living Christ was central, and miracles of healing were part of the "package."

What gives miracles their validity as a testimony of Christ? The best analogy comes from the title of Dutch Christian Corrie ten Boom's book of devotions: *Not Good If Detached*.[13] Miss ten Boom based her title from the wording sometimes found on American rail tickets, to indicate that Christian life was only valid in union with Christ. This is the issue: miracles are not separate entities in and of themselves, but are worked by the Risen Lord, to whom they point. They are indeed "not good if detached." One of the words used in the New Testament for supernatural occurrences is "sign" (*sēmeion*: a sign, mark or token). "Signs" point beyond themselves to a meaning, a deeper reality: thus, the healing points to the healer; the miraculous to the miracle-worker. Consequently,

---

11. Henderson, *From Glory to Glory*, [5–6].
12. Knowles, *New Life*, 62.
13. Ten Boom, *Not Good If Detached*.

miracles are just as valid a testimony to the living Christ in the twenty-first century as they were in the first century. They witness not only to a past event (i.e. the Resurrection of Christ) but also to the present reality of the living Christ through the power of the Holy Spirit. Indeed, that was *then*; but millions of Christians can testify that Christ is risen and active in their lives *now*. This ongoing, experiential relationship with the living Christ is the *sure foundation* for Christianity.

Bibliography

Greek terms are taken from Thayer's Greek Lexicon, Electronic Database; Hebrew terms from the Brown-Driver-Briggs Hebrew and English Lexicon, Electronic Database. Both of these are available on the Biblesoft Bible Hub website. https://www.biblehub.org/.

Arnold, Brian J. "If Christ Is Risen, Nothing Else Matters." *Phoenix Seminary* (April 12, 2020). https://ps.edu/if-christ-is-risen-nothing-else-matters/.

Bauckham, Richard. *Jesus and the Eyewitnesses: The Gospels as Eyewitness Testimony*. 2nd ed. Grand Rapids, MI: Eerdmans, 2017.

Brown, Candy Gunther. "Introduction: Pentecostalism and the Globalization of Illness and Healing." In *Global Pentecostal and Charismatic Healing*, edited by Candy Gunther Brown, with a foreword by Harvey Cox, 3–26. Oxford: University Press, 2011.

Donne John. "Meditation XVII." *Devotions upon Emergent Occasions*, 1624. Dalhousie University. https://web.cs.dal.ca/~johnston/poetry/island.html.

[Henderson, Mary]. *From Glory to Glory: A History of the Timaru New Life Centre 1960–1980*. Timaru: Dove Print, 1980.

Knowles, Brett. *New Life: A History of the New Life Churches of New Zealand 1942–1979*. 3rd ed. Lexington, KY: Emeth, 2015.

———. *Transforming Pentecostalism: The Changing Face of New Zealand Pentecostalism, 1920–2010*. Lexington, KY: Emeth, 2014.

Laurence, Sarah, et al. "Recognising Familiar Faces Out of Context." *Perception* 50.2 (February 2021) 174–77. https://journals.sagepub.com/doi/full/10.1177/0301006620984326.

Lennox, John C. *God and Stephen Hawking: Whose Design Is It Anyway?* 1st ed. Oxford: Lion, 2010.

———. *Gunning for God: Why the New Atheists Are Missing the Target*. Oxford: Lion, 2011.

———. *Miracles: Is Belief in the Supernatural Irrational?* Veritalks 2. Cambridge, MA: Veritas Forum, 2013.

Lewis, C.S. *Miracles: A Preliminary Study*. London: HarperCollins, 1947.

Stanton, Graham. *The Gospels and Jesus*. 2nd ed. Oxford Bible Series. Oxford: University Press, 2004.

BIBLIOGRAPHY

Telfer, William. "General Introduction: The Martyry." In *Cyril of Jerusalem and Nemesius of Emesa*, edited by William Telfer, 43–63. Library of Christian Classics 4. London: SCM, 1955.

Ten Boom, Corrie. *Not Good If Detached*. Fort Washington, PA: Christian Literature Crusade, 2009.

Van Voorst, Robert E. *Jesus Outside the New Testament: An Introduction to the Ancient Evidence*. Grand Rapids, MI: Eerdmans, 2000.

www.ingramcontent.com/pod-product-compliance
Lightning Source LLC
Chambersburg PA
CBHW072034060426
42449CB00010BA/2260